THE GREAT DEPRESSION

ITS IMPACT AND AMERICA'S REACTION

by Scott Gillam

PEARSON
Scott Foresman

Editorial Offices: Glenview, Illinois • Parsippany, New Jersey • New York, New York

Sales Offices: Needham, Massachusetts • Duluth, Georgia • Glenview, Illinois
Coppell, Texas • Sacramento, California • Mesa, Arizona

This photo shows the New York Stock Exchange on a busy day in the 1920s. High prices that did not reflect the true value of many stocks were one cause of the stock market crash of 1929.

Early Signs of Trouble Ahead

The popular idea that the 1920s were a time of economic growth before the **depression** of the 1930s is only partly true. The wealthy, and some in the middle class, did benefit from the rising **stock market**, where shares of companies are bought and sold, during the 1920s. Many parts of the economy, however, were depressed or getting worse throughout the same period. These included agriculture, mining, and transportation. Membership in labor unions declined sharply. Five percent of the wealthiest people owned almost half the nation's wealth, while the bottom 93 percent showed a decline in income over the final six years of the 1920s. As the gap between the wealthy and poor widened, more than half of all Americans were living below the minimum income level by the end of the 1920s.

Hard Times for Farmers

Agriculture was hit especially hard in the 1920s. Farmers had invested in machines and land to keep up with growing food demands during World War I. When the demand dropped after the war, farm prices dropped and some farmers could not keep up with payments on their loans and farms. In their effort to keep up with wartime demand, many farmers had also overworked their soil. This practice led to erosion, which further reduced the productivity of the already depleted soil. The value of farmland fell about one–third between 1920 and 1930. By 1930 the average yearly income per person for farm families was only $273. Even before the Depression, many people who had worked on farms headed toward cities, where they hoped to find jobs in industry. Many industries, however, were not hiring workers, as many machines replaced humans.

The Roaring Twenties

After World War I ended, wages in the United States were good, food prices were low, prices on the stock market were rising, and there were many new goods people wanted to buy. It was very easy to borrow money to buy shares in companies on the stock market. Many people paid for some of the shares and borrowed money to buy the rest. These people hoped to pay off the loan when the stock rose and they could sell it for a profit. They knew this was a period of stock price inflation. As long as stock prices were going up, however, people felt safe. When enough people realized that these high prices did not reflect the stocks' true value, however, the prices went down sharply. Others then had to sell to pay off those from whom they had borrowed, and prices fell further. This was how the stock market **crash** started.

The 1920s saw many new consumer goods on the market. Loans made it easier to own such items, as long as the payments were made.

Many farmers joined a vast group of people who sought work in the fruit and vegetable farms of the West Coast.

Farming During the Great Depression

The stock market crash, caused partly by buying on borrowed money, was the first sign of an economic depression that was to last from 1929 until 1941. The Great Depression, as it came to be called, was a period in which business investment almost disappeared. During this period, the value of goods and services produced dropped almost one third and **unemployment** rose to almost 25 percent. Agriculture, which employed almost one–quarter of the population in 1934, was hit especially hard. Farm prices, which had been depressed since the 1920s, were not helped by the drought that hit much of the Midwest and Southwest during the 1930s. Some farmers abandoned their farms completely and headed west, hoping to find work on the West Coast as **migrant workers**.

From Boom to Bust

As business declined, jobs disappeared, and farms suffered, many people had only their savings, their family and friends, and private charity to support them. President Herbert Hoover appealed to business to make new investments in order to create jobs. He did not believe in direct handouts of money or other aid to those in need. Hoover believed such help would make people too dependent on government and would discourage self-sufficiency.

During the worst part of the Depression, people without jobs and money had to wait in long lines to be fed by private charities.

People who could not pay their rent or loans on their houses moved in with relatives or traveled in search of work, hoping to survive as best as they could. Some even used scrap materials to build their own homes, groups of which were called "Hoovervilles." People who needed money were sometimes forced to sell their belongings. Former businessmen could be seen selling apples for five cents each. Most people, of course, still had jobs and homes. For those who did not, however, times were hard.

The Coming of the New Deal

Franklin Delano Roosevelt defeated Herbert Hoover to become President in 1933. Unlike Hoover, Roosevelt believed that government had a vital role to play in fighting the Depression. Roosevelt's New Deal consisted of many programs designed to improve the economy in three ways. To bring relief to people without jobs, the government provided temporary work, such as repairing roads and bridges. To improve the economy's recovery, the government planned big projects, such as building dams and other construction projects. To reform

the stock market, the government created the Securities and Exchange Commission. The commission is a government agency that supervises the stock market.

The major New Deal programs were called relief, recovery, and reform programs. Relief programs provided immediate action to keep the economy from getting worse. One relief program was the Civilian Conservation Corps. The Civilian Conservation Corps (CCC) provided temporary jobs that helped save land and forests. Recovery programs were designed to improve the economy. They included the Works Progress Administration and the Home Owners Loan Corporation. The Works Progress Administration (WPA) provided long-term jobs building roads, schools, and dams. The Home Owners Loan Corporation gave loans to homeowners so they could pay back bank loans on their homes. Reform programs such as Social Security were meant to avoid future economic disasters. The Social Security Administration provides monthly payments to senior citizens.

Roosevelt was the first President to make full use of radio to get his message across to the general public, both through formal speeches and informal "fireside chats."

The Great Depression Continues

Roosevelt's first term, from 1933 to 1937, was widely considered successful. The banks reopened, the nation's production improved, and employment went up due to the public jobs program. Congress was willing to approve the great majority of Roosevelt's proposed programs because of his great personal popularity. Both Roosevelt and his wife, Eleanor, proved to be tireless supporters of New Deal programs around the country. Hope was in the air, but this mood of optimism proved to be very difficult to maintain. The huge economic problems of the Depression were proving too stubborn for any one person to solve.

By 1937 the New Deal had begun to show signs of failure. Unemployment began to increase again.

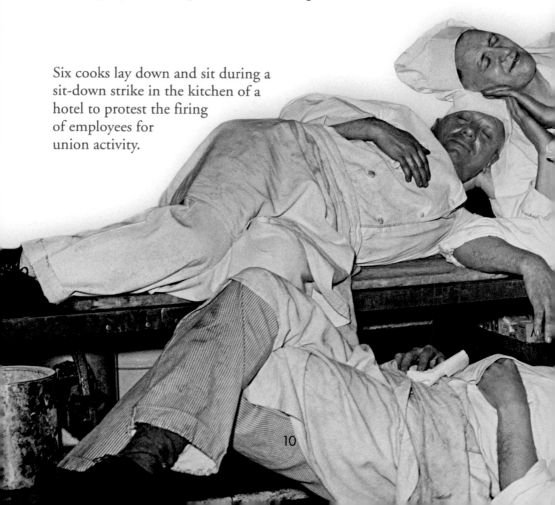

Six cooks lay down and sit during a sit-down strike in the kitchen of a hotel to protest the firing of employees for union activity.

Nervous workers began to form unions to try to preserve their jobs and working conditions. A new labor tactic, the sit-down strike, was successful in the workplace but was declared unconstitutional by the Supreme Court. In a sit-down strike, workers take over their workplace but refuse to work. By occupying their workplace, strikers discourage their employer from hiring replacement workers. Roosevelt's plan to expand the Supreme Court to create a majority favorable to his ideas was also defeated. Only the economic growth created by World War II finally broke the grip of the Depression on the United States.

Entertainment and American Concerns

During the Depression, Americans sought
entertainment that would not only help them
escape their worries but inspire them to deal with
their problems. For example, gangster movies in the
1930s helped viewers understand how greed could
harm society. At the same time, audiences could get
satisfaction from seeing   the criminal punished.
Musicals, on the other hand, were often meant
to inspire hope by showing how determination
and luck could lead to success. This theme of
persistence in the face of great odds was seen in the
real-life story of Seabiscuit, an awkward racehorse
who was the unexpected victor in a celebrated
race with War Admiral in 1938. Toward the end
of the decade, serious films such as *Stagecoach* and
The Grapes of Wrath illustrated how sharing and
cooperation were necessary if communities were to
meet the challenges they faced. *The Grapes of Wrath*,
adapted from the novel by John Steinbeck, told the
story of farmers during the Depression who had to
stick together to survive.

Many people escaped
their worries by
going to the movies.

The Depression and Its Impact

Japan's invasion of China in 1937 and Hitler's attack on Poland in 1939 caused the United States to begin the preparations for war that revived the economy enough to finally end the Depression. The nation's main enemy was now the Axis powers overseas rather than economic depression at home. Unemployment fell dramatically toward the end of the 1930s, as new warships and airplanes were built and arms orders were received from England and France. With the Japanese attack on Pearl Harbor in December 1941, the United States officially declared war and the Depression unofficially ended.

These workers benefited from the United States' preparations for World War II. From 1939 to 1940, unemployment fell by 4 million, as the nation built more ships and airplanes.

American lives today are different because of New Deal programs that still exist, such as Social Security, federal housing, and welfare. The New Deal idea of borrowing huge amounts of money to fight big problems, such as economic depression, was also supported by many people for projects such as the arms race during the Cold War. In such cases, however, the nation has struggled with huge debts that make spending for other worthwhile projects much more difficult. The impact of the Depression can be felt today in both expected and unexpected ways.

Glossary

crash a sudden and severe decline in business

depression a period of severe decline in an economy

migrant worker a worker who travels from one place to another in search of work

stock market an organized market where stocks are bought and sold

unemployment the number of workers who are without jobs